G000016053

Thanks to Muz, Gruz, Dmunger and all our customers and friends on Broadway Market for your help.

First Published 2019 by Modesty Designs Ltd (T/A Quite Good Cards)
5 Cornfield Terrace, Eastbourne,
East Sussex, BN21 4NN, United Kingdom
www.QuiteGoodCards.com

Copyright © The Ward Brothers, 2019
Illustrations by Eddie Ward
Printed and bound by CPI Group (UK) Ltd, Croydon, CR0 4YY

ISBN 978-1-5272-4159-6

The right of The Ward Brothers to be identified as the authors of this work has been asserted by them in accordance with the Copyright, Designs and Patents act of 1988.

CELEBRITY PUNS

TWISTED POPULAR CULTURE

QUITE GOOD CARDS

Thank you so much for buying our book! We do hope you have a splendid time giggling your way through our twisted celebrity world.

With the help of our customers on Broadway Market and our fabulous stockists we have been able to create these punderful illustrations since 2014.

On our website, QuiteGoodCards.com, we also sell prints, T-shirts and of course our greeting cards. All the designs featured in this book are there in one form or another so please feel free to give us a visit.

All that is left to say is another big thank you for supporting us and if you would like keep up to date with our work you can follow us on Instagram, Facebook and Twitter.

Have a good one!

The Ward Brothers

ADELE BOY

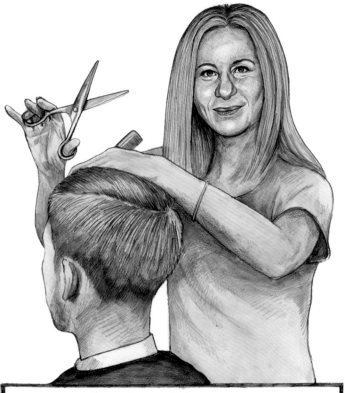

BARBER STREISAND

BATNAN

BENEDICT

CUMBERPATCH

BEYONCE BOWLS

BRUCE SPRING CLEAN

CATE BLANKET

CHANNING

TANTRUM

CHRISTIAN

BALE

CLARE BALDING

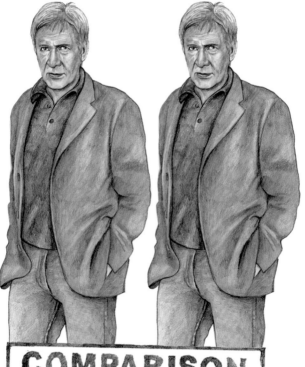

COMPARISON

FORD

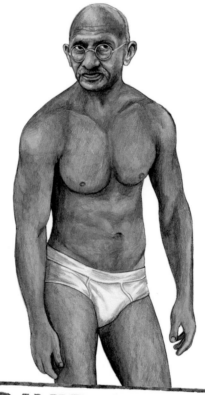

DAVID GANDHI

DIPLOMA FAITH

DOLLY SPARTAN

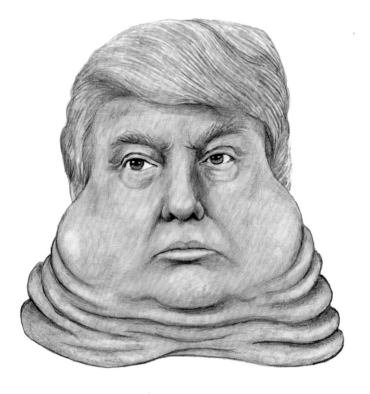

DONALD LUMP

DRAKE O'MALFOY

EGG SHEERAN

ELFISH PRESLEY

ELLEN DEGENEROUS

FAT DAMON

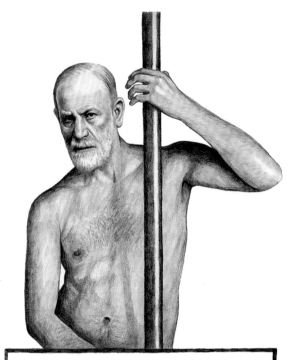

FREUDIAN STRIP

GEORGE LOONEY

GWYNETH POULTRY

HARRY PILES

HARRY PORTER

HELEN MERINGUE

HELENA
BONO CARTER

HUGE JACKMAN

JENNIFER
LOW-RES

JEREMY IRONS

J. K. ROLLING

JOHN
TRA-VAULTER

JOHNNY DEEP

JUDI HENCH

JUSTIN BEAVER

KANYE PEST

KATE LIDLTON

KIM JONG-UNO

KURT CORBYN

KYLIE MIN-OGRE

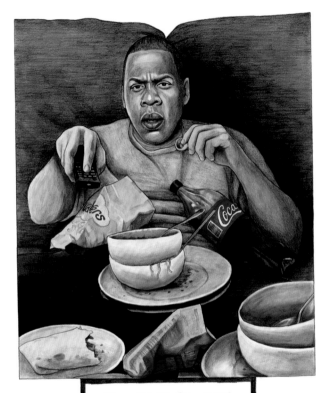

LAY Z

LIONEL MESSY

MADONNER

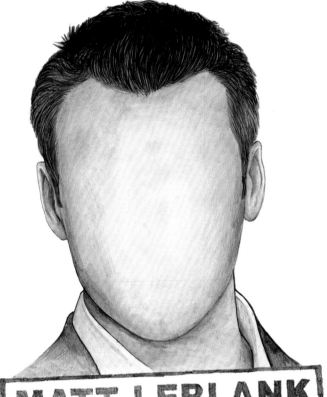

MATT LEBLANK

MEGHAN MERKEL

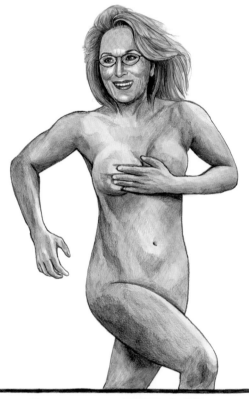

MERYL STREAK

MR TEA

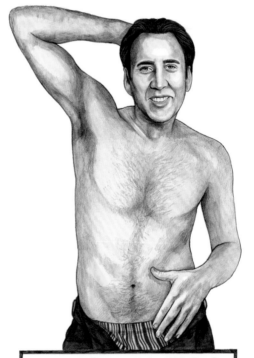

NIPPLELESS

CAGE

OLDERMORT

OPERA WINFREY

ORLANDO BROOM

OWL PACINO

PIERCE BROSNAN

PROM CRUISE

QUEEN

REESE WITH A SPOON

RUSSELL CROW

RYAN GOSLING

SAMUEL L. JACKSON

SCARLETT

NO HANDS SON

SCHOFELD

SIMON TROWEL

GO AHEAD, MAKE MY DAY!

SKINT EASTWOOD

SLIM

KARDASHIAN

SLING

SNOOD LAW

STEPHEN FRY

STEVEN STEALBERG

STEVIE WONDER

TAILOR SWIFT

THE FROCK

UBER THURMAN

VAN GOTH

TOM THANKS

ILLUSTRATED BY
EDDIE WARD